STOCK MAGNATE

A BLUEPRINT TO MAKE MONEY CONSISTENTLY FROM THE STOCK MARKET

By
Karthik Kuppuswamy

Copyright © 2017 Karthik Kuppuswamy

Publishing Services by Happy Self Publishing
www.happyselfpublishing.com

Year: 2017

All rights reserved. No reproduction, transmission or copy of this publication can be made without the written consent of the author in accordance with the provision of the Copyright Acts. Any person doing so will be liable to civil claims and criminal prosecution.

Happy Self Publishing.

Disclaimer

This book is for informational and educational purposes only and does not constitute an offer to sell or offers a solicitation of an offer to buy any security which may be referenced in the book. The information provided in the book is for personal, non-commercial and educational use. This book does not provide investment advice and does not represent that the securities or services discussed are suitable for any investor. Investors are advised not to rely on any information contained in the book in the process of making a fully informed investment decision.

This book may include market analysis. All ideas, opinions, and/or forecasts, expressed or implied herein, information, charts or examples contained in the lessons, are for informational and educational purposes only and should not be construed as a recommendation to invest, trade, and/or speculate in the markets. Any investments, trades, and/or speculations made in light of the ideas, opinions, and/or forecasts, expressed or implied herein, are committed at your own risk, financial or otherwise.

This Book does not render tax or legal advice. The information found in this book does not make any offer to solicit, deal in, sell or dispose of any security for valuable consideration, and does not make any advisement in the furtherance of an order to buy or sell a security. The use of this book is for informational and educational purposes only and does not constitute advice in any form in the furtherance of any trade or trading decisions. The accuracy, completeness and timeliness of the information contained in this book cannot be guaranteed. For various reasons no proof of documents will be given. Past performance doesn't guarantee future results. This book does not warranty, guarantee or make any representations, or assume any liability with regard to financial results based on the use of the information in the book.

This book has links to and from many websites for the convenience and benefit of the user. News, views, opinions, recommendations and other information obtained from sources outside of this book and used in this book are believed to be reliable, but I cannot guarantee their accuracy or completeness. All such information is subject to change at any time without notice. This book assumes no responsibility for the content of any links. The fact that such links may exist does not indicate approval or endorsement of any material contained on any linked sites. Past performance will not and does not guarantee future performance. Readers and Investors are advised to make logical and competent decisions that they are solely responsible for.

Dedication

I want to dedicate this book to all traders and investors; who want to start trading or who are losing money trading the stock market.

Acknowledgement

I would like to thank all the stock market traders, mentors, market wizards, fictional and real characters, authors, and bloggers from around the world from whom I have learned from. Namely, Jesse Livermore, William O'Neil, Vince Stanzione, Bruce Wayne, Adam Khoo, Sam Rogers, John Tuld, Jack D Schwager, Dr. Van Tharp, and others.

Table of Contents

Disclaimer v

Dedication vii

Acknowledgement ix

Glossary of Terms & Phrases xiii

Chapter 1: Introduction to Stock Trading 1

Chapter 2: What's Your Edge; Do You Have Any? 25

Chapter 3: Position Sizing 49

Chapter 4: Psychology and Emotions 61

Chapter 5: Contingencies and Risks 71

Conclusion 77

Glossary of Terms & Phrases

STOCK: Stock is a type of security that signifies the ownership in a corporation. It represents a claim on part of the corporation's assets and earnings.

STOCK MARKET: Stock Market is where the issuing, buying and selling of equities (Stocks of publicly traded companies) takes place.

FUNDAMENTAL ANALYSIS: Is a method of evaluating stocks or other securities in an attempt to measure its intrinsic value. This is done by examining related economic, financial and other qualitative and quantitative factors.

TECHNICAL ANALYSIS: Is the financial analysis that uses chart patterns in market data to identify trends and make predictions.

STRATEGY: A method that uses Technical or Fundamental analysis or both to buy a stock.

SCREENER: A Screener is a tool used by traders and investors used to filter for stocks based on predetermined criteria.

BULL MARKET: A market where the price is going up overtime, making higher lows and higher highs.

BEAR MARKET: A market where the price is going down overtime, making lower lows and lower highs.

FOREX: Forex is the short form for Foreign Exchange; trading different currency pairs like EUR/USD, GBP/CAD, USD/JPY, AUD/USD etc.

LEVERAGE: Leverage is when you use borrowed capital, expecting the profits to be higher than the interest, this could yield in high losses as well.

COMPOUND INTEREST: Compound Interest is calculated on the initial principal amount and the accumulated interest on the previous periods of the deposits

SWING TRADE: A trade that lasts anywhere between a few days to a few months.

DAY TRADE: A trade that lasts anywhere between a few minutes to a few days.

ROULETTE MINIMUM BET SIZE: On a roulette table, there will have a minimum bet size, below which the player will not be allowed to place bets.

ROULETTE MAXIMUM BET SIZE: On a roulette table, there will have a maximum bet size, above which the player will not be allowed to place bets.

STOPLOSS ORDER: A Stoploss order is an advance order to sell an asset once a set price point (The price where you decide to get out if you were wrong) has been reached; when you are long or have a buy position A Stoploss order is placed below the opening price, and if the price starts to fall you will not lose more than the preset level.

TAKEPROFIT ORDER: A Takeprofit order is placed above the opening price so once the price reaches the preset level, the order will be closed at a profit.

FIBONACCI NUMBERS: Fibonacci numbers starts with 0, followed by a one, and the next number will be derived by adding the previous two numbers. They are as follows: 0,1,1,2,3,5,8,13 etc...

SMA or Simple Moving Average: Is a widely used indicator in technical analysis that helps smooth out price action by filtering out the "noise" from random price fluctuations.

EMA or Exponential Moving Average: It is a type of moving average, where more weight is given to the latest data. It reacts faster to recent price changes, than a Simple Moving Average.

SUPPORT AND RESISTANCE: In trading support and resistance is a concept, where the price of an asset tends to stop and reverse, this is because the buyers or sellers have taken control over the other. It can be a Moving Average, Trendline etc. This is represented by multiple touches (Touching the support or resistance line more than once). Support is below the price level and resistance is above the price level.

RETRACEMENT: Is a temporary reversal in the direction of a stock's price that goes against the prevailing trend. It does not signify a change in the larger trend.

R: 'R' stands for Risk and Reward. In my trading business, 1R is represented by 1% of my equity. E.g. you risk 1R to make 3R:

What this means is you are risking 1% to make 3%. So the Risk:Reward ratio would be 1:3.

Spread betting and CFD (Contracts for Difference): Trading vehicles or methods that use leverage to amplify profits and losses.

NOTE FROM THE AUTHOR

Hi, I am Karthik ; I have been trading stocks for the last 6 years. And making money consistently trading the markets has not been a straightforward journey. There are various elements that I had to learn and understand the hard way for me to be successful. Now I am able to see my account grow steadily overtime. I am sharing my journey with you how I transformed from a Rookie to Pro trader. I want you to achieve the same level of success that I did, the fast track way. There are three factors that are essential to becoming a successful trader: 20% of your success comes from your strategy or method used to buy a stock, 30% from how you control your position sizing and 50% from your own psychology and emotions. In this book, I cover all the three factors that you need to be a successfully profitable trader. By the end of this book, you will also be able to use the knowledge and experience to make money consistently from the stock market.

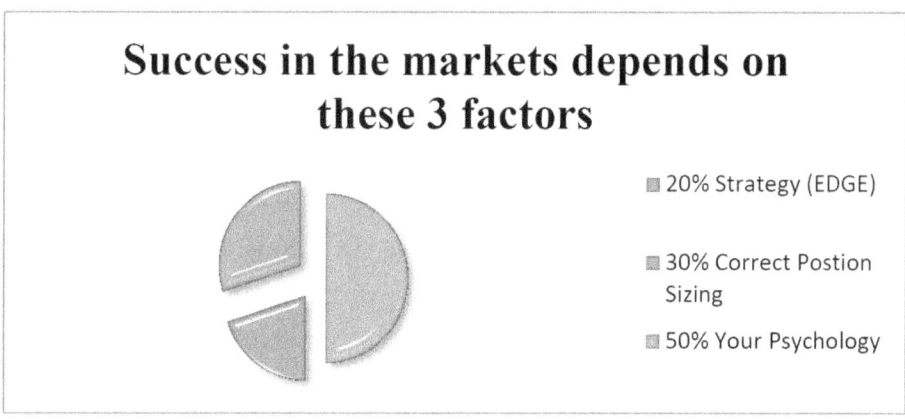

The first thing you need to know is that 90% of people trading stocks lose money. The primary reason is that they do not have their objectives in place. Most people don't even treat trading as a business. They are made to believe it is as easy as clicking a few buttons, and in other cases, they are made to believe that only hedge funds, banks, and large institutions make money. And

Rookie traders buy stocks based on tips, emotions, and broker recommendation. They can be right, sometimes, but you will never make money consistently.

I want to aid you to achieve your long-term objectives in good times and bad. You are going to be making mistakes, and not all trades will go in your favor. I want to help you start thinking in terms of probability and expectancy. I do this by sharing the strategies I use to pick stocks and manage them. I make money consistently by feeding my winners and starving my losing stocks. Before you step into the world's largest Casino (i.e. The Stock Market), I want to load you up with all the ammunition and strategies that will make you money when times are good and defend you when times are tough. It doesn't end here; you can always get in touch with me on stockmagnatebook@gmail.com. I will be more than happy to answer your questions.

Stocks and Stock Markets throughout the world are very similar. The underlying reasons for a stock to go up or down in price is Greed and Fear, which are present across the globe. When more people get greedy, they want more of the stock; the price of the stock will go up, and when more people are fearful; they want to get rid of the stock, so the price of the stock goes down. And between the peak and valley of these emotions, there is a lot of money to be made and lost. Our aim is to identify which stage we are in and to funnel the money slowly into our accounts.

THE STOCK MARKET IS A DEVICE FOR TRANSFERRING MONEY FROM THE IMPATIENT TO THE PATIENT.

-WARREN BUFFET

There are many U.S Stocks featured in this book. That does not mean the strategies and concepts wouldn't fit other stocks in other markets across the world. The principles and screeners can be used across any stock in any market across the world. So you can use these concepts to fit the timing and market in which you are trading. The fundamental reason businesses and people throughout the world are very similar is both have to be profitable, there should be big money flowing into the stock to drive the price up, supported by strong fundamentals. So keep an open mind from whichever part of the world you are from. As a trader, you have to think globally and act locally. There are consistently profitable traders across the world, trading various instruments in various markets.

- Rookie – A trader who is not making money consistently.
- Pro – A trader who is making money consistently when times are good, and protecting his/her capital when times are tough.

Chapter 1

Introduction to Stock Trading

1A: WHY I STARTED TRADING:

There are many different reasons why people start trading stocks, forex, commodities, bonds, indices, ETF's, etc. For me, it was the subprime crisis, which took place between 2008-2009. When I was just about to graduate, the newspapers, TV, and other media sources were all posting really bad news, as if the world we know was about to end. It was really depressing during this time. Companies started firing people left, right, and center. So for me to get a job in the UK was practically impossible. This really intrigued me, so I started investigating the reasons why this was happening and wanted to understand the markets and how they functioned.

The other reason may sound a bit shallow, but... well I am just going to share it. Walking down Canary Warf, London, I saw men in well-tailored suits driving really fancy cars. I really wanted to know the reason behind such great wealth. TV shows and movies glamorized traders. So I called a friend who was a commodities trader and asked him "How do I start trading in markets?" His answer was a bit vague, and he said, "it's complicated." But this was not a reason to stop me. I have always believed if someone else could do it, so can I.

Like most teenagers, I was cash tight. However, this did not stop me from opening an account. I couldn't fund my account with $100,000; I had only $2,000 to start with. Well, in the markets, starting with such low capital, the room to trade what I wanted was limited. So I started trading forex as the leverage was 1:500. So did I make my $2,000 into $1,000,000? The answer is no, in fact, I blew it in a matter of weeks. This left me devastated. It was my living expenses for the next 3 months. This really affected my psychology, and I felt like a loser. Now, with no money, my option left was to open a demo account.

These reasons were not enough to keep me off the screens. I started reading anything that I could get a hold of about the markets. This included books and watching many videos of top traders; why they succeeded and what mistakes they made. Slowly, I was able to start painting a mental picture of what markets were and what products each of these traders traded. This made me realize how trading has so much to do with personality, strategy, markets, and methodology.

Trading stocks is one of the businesses that gives you a sense of freedom, you can literally trade with just an iPad and an internet connection. Freedom to do this sitting in any part of the globe was one of the other reasons I got into trading. And, this is one of those businesses that anyone can do, a Janitor or a billionaire, the rules of the game are same. This doesn't mean everyone who trades is going to be successful. Hopefully, by the end of this book, I can show how this is possible, and I'll give you all the tools and strategies that are required for success in trading the markets.

Another reason why I started trading was I wanted to have a secondary source of income. If I learned how to make money in the markets, then I could put my primary source of income into trading for it to compound.

"THE MOST POWERFUL FORCE IN THE UNIVERSE IS COMPOUND INTEREST. COMPOUND INTEREST IS THE EIGHTH WONDER OF THE WORLD. HE, WHO UNDERSTANDS IT, EARNS IT AND HE WHO DOESN'T PAYS IT."

ALBERT EINSTEIN

There is a small story that could help you understand the power of compound interest even better. Once upon a time, there was a village boy who fell in love with a princess. The King was not happy with this, so he offered the boy whatever he wanted to stay away from his daughter. The boy agreed to the offer and said he wanted a dollar, and it had to double every month for the rest of his life. They king was an honorable man, so he granted his wish. The first month the boy had $1, the second month he had $2, the third month he had $4.... Look at the chart below.

STOCK MAGNATE

1st month	1 dollar
2nd month	2 dollars
3rd month	4 dollars
4th month	8 dollars
5th month	16 dollars
6th month	32 dollars
7th month	64 dollars
8th month	128 dollars
9th month	250 dollars
10th month	500 dollars
11th month	1000 dollars
12th month	2000 dollars
13th month	4000 dollars
14th month	8000 dollars
15th month	16000 dollars
16th month	32000 dollars
17th month	64000 dollars
18th month	128000 dollars
19th month	250000 dollars
20th month	500000 dollars
21st month	1000000 dollars

After this point, the king gave everything to the boy. The boy then asked if he could marry the king's daughter. The king was more than happy to get his daughter married to a millionaire. The point of the story is that the power of compounding interest can make you a millionaire over time.

These were the reasons why and what that kept me motivated to trade the markets, even after blowing up my account more than a few times. However, I had not achieved consistency, and the road to reaching my goal was really unclear. Truthfully, I did not know what my goal was, I was still a rookie.

1B: What are your Objectives? Here are mine.

The transition phase from a rookie to a Pro starts with defining your objectives. So define your Objectives, now. This may sound difficult, but without knowing what they are, do not go ahead to the next chapter. Start defining them, if you find it difficult to define them, maybe you can pick up some valid goals and objectives from mine. The other reason why I say defining your objectives is important is because this is where you draw the line between a gambler, who is in the markets for fun, and a trader who is here to make consistent money. Are you here to be right, or are you here to make money?

So, here are my Objectives:

1. I am an equity (stock) swing trader. I trade the stocks that have the highest probability of going up. I use proven existing strategies and the ones that I have personally developed. These methods of screening and selecting stocks fit my personality. I treat trading as a business; I am not here to prove that I am right or to gamble. I trade only in the direction of the prevailing trend. I know I cannot

control the markets; the only thing I know I can control in my trading business is my risk.

2. I would like to risk a maximum of 1% in a stock. If I have $10,000 in my account, the maximum I will risk in one stock is $100. I do this so that a single position doesn't affect me. I get about 0 – 5 stock notifications that meet my screening criteria every day. And I want to have enough trading capital to buy the stocks when these notifications come. You will learn more about this in the 2nd Chapter. For new traders, I really recommend risking about 0.25% to 0.50% of your account, just to get a feel of trading.

3. My cumulative risk of all the open positions should be maximum 10%. With 1% risk on each position, I can open a maximum 10 position. Why I have such a high limit is because, in the stock markets, anything can happen anytime. So if all my positions go against me, the maximum I will lose is about $1,000. In the past, there have been many Bear markets that last a few weeks to years, such as the ones in 1637, 1797, 1819, 1837, 1857, 1884, 1901, 1907, 1929, 1937, 1974, 1987, 1992, 1997, 2000, and the most recent was in 2008 (subprime crisis). There will be many more of these crashes to come. And these crashes don't tell you when they are coming. You cannot control it, slow it, or stop it. You can just react. You will make a lot of money if you were right or get left behind if you were wrong. There will always be winners and losers, happy sides and sad sides, Fat Cats and Starving Dogs.

Imagine if you had open positions risking more than 10% and all the positions went against you. Could you digest and take such big hit on your equity? What is the maximum drawdown you can digest? Look at the table below and clearly analyze what sort of emotions you'd be feeling with each of them.

Table 1

Drawdown	Gain to Recovery
10%	11.1%
20%	25%
30%	42.9%
40%	66.7%
50%	100%
60%	150%
90%	900%

i.e. When you lose 10% of your account you need to make back 11.1% from the markets; when you lose 90% of your account, you'd need to make 900% from the markets to get back to your starting equity balance. So don't lose money by risking too much at any point of time. Suppose your starting balance is $10,000, and if you lose $1,000 (i.e. a 10% drop in your equity), your account balance would now be $10,000 - $1,000 = $9,000. You need to make 11.1% of $9,000 to get back to $10,000. And if you lose 90% of your capital i.e. $10,000 - $9,000 =$1,000 you need to make 900% of $1,000 to get back to your starting capital of $10,000.

4. I would like to grow my equity at 30 to 50% a year. You may ask, how is it even possible to achieve this with such tight risk? The answer lies in the magic of position sizing.

The mathematics of what you risk to reward is the basis of such a level of growth that you can expect from properly executed position sizing models. I will explain more about this in detail in Chapter 3. I risk 1% or 1R to make 3% or 3R or more. So even if I am only 50% right, I still make money. (Here "R" represents the unit Risk and unit Reward, I will explain more about this in Chapter 3: Position sizing). **In my trading business, 1R represents 1% risk.**

So imagine, I risk 1R in 1 stock, and I have a total of 10 open positions. So, 10R risk for 10 stocks.

50% of the time I'm right (when I am right, 5 of my stocks will return 3R each, which is 15R profit).

50% of the time I'm wrong (when I am wrong, 5 of my stocks will lose 1R each, which is 5R loss).

So the net profit is 15R -5R =10R profit. (When I am trading 1R =1% of my equity.)

YOU GET RECESSIONS, YOU HAVE STOCK MARKET DECLINES. IF YOU DON'T UNDERSTAND THAT'S GOING TO HAPPEN THEN YOU'RE NOT READY, YOU WON'T DO WELL IN THE MARKETS.

-PETER LYNCH

1C. UNDERSTANDING THE BUSINESS OF A CASINO

If you want to make money consistently in the stock markets, then you will need to understand and learn the business model of a casino. The closest business model that can be related to trading is the business of a casino. We are going to use the game of roulette as the example. The question that will pass through your head is how roulette is even remotely related to trading. Look at the similarities and differences.

Similarities	Differences
There is no one to hold your hand while you place the bets or when you trade.	You can bend the rules in trading to meet your objective. On the roulette table, the casino predefines the rules. So you cannot bend them.
No set combination or rules. You can bet on anything, anytime within the table limit on roulette, and you can trade all of your money on any of the stocks available.	You can set larger winners in trading, e.g. 3 to 5 times your risk. But in roulette when you can only double your money or lose it on any bet.
Both can be really addictive and you can try both on demo accounts.	Trading can be longer term, where you place a trade where it can take care of itself whether a win or lose. Roulette is time-based. i.e. the time for the ball to land on a number.

The stock market is the largest Casino in the world." You might think that you'll lose money when in a Casino. Think again, do all people in a casino lose money? Instead of being the player who gambles, what if it was the other way around and you were the owner of the casino. Wouldn't you be happy? Have you heard the phrase "The house always wins"? How? Let's find out.

Why does the player lose over the long run and the casino makes money in a game of chance? This is because; the casino has the edge over the players. They do this by bending the rules of the game to their advantage, where they have a statistical edge over the players; this is called the house edge. In other words, they have a positive expectancy over the players. There are many games that players can play in a casino. The example I am going to show you is the game of Roulette. If you have not played this game before, I recommend that you download a free app and try it for yourself. Make sure it's a demo account, and DO NOT play with real money.

<u>The Game of Roulette</u>

In the game of Roulette, there are numbers from 1 to 36, and in addition to that, there are the green numbers 0 & 00. So a total of 36 +2= 38 numbers to bet on. You can place a bet on any of the numbers, BLACK or RED, ODD or EVEN, 1 TO 18, 19 TO 36, 1 TO

12, 13 TO 24, 25 TO 36. There are various combinations of bets that you can choose from. Please look at the table below. Once the dealer spins the ball, and if the ball lands on the number you bet on, you win, else you lose (it's a win for the casino). Many people think that when they place a bet, they have a 50:50 chance that they will win. However, this isn't correct. There are 18 RED & 18 BLACK; there are 18 EVEN and 18 ODD numbers and 2 greens (0 &00), so the total number of numbers on the roulette table is 38. The 2 green numbers added to the roulette wheel is how the casino gets its edge over the players. This is called the house edge. Let's look at the calculations below.

Example: If you bet on RED (18 numbers)

The chance of winning for the player is 18/38 (since there are 38 numbers in total) = 47.37%

The chance of winning for the Casino is 20/38 (If the ball falls on green numbers, the casino wins) = 52.63%

So the player's edge is 47.37%, and the casino's edge is 52.63%, so the casino has a 5.26% edge over the players. Let's look at what this 5.26% edge equates to in the long haul.

Look at the table below to find the house edge

BET	PAYS	PROBABILITY	HOUSE EDGE
RED	1	47.37%	5.26%
BLACK	1	47.37%	5.26%
ODD	1	47.37%	5.26%
EVEN	1	47.37%	5.26%
1 TO 18	1	47.37%	5.26%
19 TO 36	1	47.37%	5.26%

1 TO 12	2	31.58%	5.26%
13 TO 24	2	31.58%	5.26%
25 TO 36	2	31.58%	5.26%
SIX LINE (6 NUMBERS)	5	15.79%	5.26%
FIRST FIVE (5 NUMBERS)	6	13.16%	5.26%
CORNER (4 NUMBERS)	8	10.53%	7.89%
STREET (3 NUMBERS)	11	7.89%	5.26%
SPLIT (2 NUMBERS)	17	5.26%	5.26%
ANY ONE NUMBER	35	2.63%	5.26%

There is a something called a table limit, meaning there is a minimum bet size and a maximum bet size. This ensures that the bets placed by the player are broken down into smaller chunks. The casinos usually have this because they don't want any 1 hand in which they could lose money. Example, the martingale system, in theory, works because you just keep doubling your bet until you win. But the casino knows that, so they won't allow you to bet over a certain limit, which is set on the table. There is a minimum bet size as well. This is to ensure that you have a limited number of rounds from the minimum bet size to the maximum bet size; to ensure their edge is always maintained. You will get a better idea once you start playing on a demo account.

Try now:

1st open a demo account on any of the free roulette apps and fund it with $10,000 play money; your task is to try to make it to $1,000,000, which you will never be able to; the point is you have to try and fail.

2nd try various combinations of bets to get the hang of it.

3rd start with the smallest bet size and double it every time you lose, then try the same with every win. Start again with the smallest bet size, add 1 every time you lose, then try the same with every win. See if you are able to stick to this position sizing model. If not, write down the reasons why.

4th you should play the game until you realize that it is never possible to make money in the long run since the odds are in the casino's favor. Gambling can be fun; don't ever think that you will be a millionaire playing the game of roulette unless you are a billionaire.

For every $1 bet on EVEN or ODD, RED or BLACK on a roulette table, the casino makes 5.26% of that = 0.052cents. (In the short term, the casino may not win every round, but in the long run, the statistics are in the casino's favor. So over the long-term, they make their money.) So if $100,000 is bet over 1,000 rounds, the casino will make 5.26% of $100,000 = $5,260. So the more people who bet, the more the casino makes. That is why, in Las Vegas, Casino's offer free rooms, free food & drinks, and lots of entertainment. After all, drunk players are good for business.

Calculations to demonstrate the edge.

1,000 bets @ $100/bet = $100,000 (The total volume bet)

Casino's edge (52.63%) & Player's edge (47.37%), e.g. for the 1,000 bets, 52.63% of the time the casino wins and 47.37% of the time the player wins. So, 526.3 rounds the casino wins and 473.7 rounds the player wins.

526.3*$100 (average bet size) = $52,630 (for the casino), and 473.7*$100 (average bet size) = $ 47,370 (for the player).

$52,630 - $47,370 = $5,260.

I hope you understand the above calculations, it is essential that you learn how the casinos make money. Only then, will you be able to apply this to stock trading. Stock trading is not as straightforward as the above calculation. It involves a bit more than this; I'm going to try to explain this for you to understand. Once you understand the basic concepts and start thinking in terms of probabilities and statistics, then you will be able to apply the calculation to make money consistently in the stock markets.

In the following chapters, I will show you my edge, how I use the position sizing strategy that fits my personality and how it keeps my psychology in check. When I started, I never knew any of this. You are literally on the fast track of understanding these concepts, which will enable you to make money consistently in the markets. It will then become a mechanical process. Remember, good trading is boring. If you are here for some fun and excitement, trading is not for you.

When you buy a stock without doing any research, the outcome will be really random. Meaning it has a 50% chance it will go up and 50% chance it will go down. Well, this is not really that bad. Using proper position sizing, you can be profitable even with these odds. But when your emotions such as greed, fear, hope, and excitement are taken consideration, the odds of making money reduce drastically.

In a casino, you bet $1 to make $1, so your win-loss ratio is 1:1. But, in the stock market, when you don't have a strategy, proper position sizing strategy, and your emotions in check, you will lose more when you are wrong and make less when you are right. This is what Rookies face on a day-to-day basis.

Let's look at some examples.

You buy a stock at $20 after seeing the news or getting a tip-off from your friend, the internet, or from a market guru. Thinking you will be a millionaire overnight you put all your trading equity into it, i.e. more than you could handle if it went against you. And guess what, the stock goes to $10. You have just wiped out 50% of your entire capital. Please look at TABLE 1 above to understand your drawdown to recovery. Some traders will still be holding on to this position and will console themselves saying this is a long-term investment. Don't do that. When it comes to trading, there is an old Wall Street saying, "Hope is for the hopeless."

The market doesn't care who you are or where you're from or how long you have worked to save this money. But then, if it went the way you hoped, to about $22, now you are profitable, then the fear kicks in saying you could lose the money. Or this could be because you wanted instant gratification. So you take small profits. Looking at both scenarios, you can let your losses run, or you can cut your profits short. And with 50% odds, just do the math. This is an underlying factor why rookies lose money, and it's the exact opposite of a Pro trader. I want to help you let your winners run and cut your losers by showing you the methods I use when entering a trade.

You always start by asking the question, how much can I lose if this trade goes against me? Am I sticking to my objectives? The way I control my risk is by having a STOPLOSS and TAKEPROFIT orders in place before entering, always. Without these two orders, I think you are just like a gambler looking to have fun. And, I don't like big fat losses, they just destroy confidence in trading. As a pro, which you are going to be by the end of the book, we always make money. We do this by replicating the business model of a casino. Think of yourself as the owner of the casino, you will learn how to bend the rules to have better odds so that the more you trade, the more money you make.

As a Pro, you have to buy stocks that meet only the most stringent criteria to increase your edge in the markets. We look for patterns that have high probability low-risk entry points. These stocks have to be fundamentally strong with strong technical signs. I call this method of screening "The FUNTECH method," which is short for Fundamental + Technical.

1D. STOCK MARKET STAGES AND TIMINGS

This is where the interesting part begins. The stock market is like the ocean, constantly changing. There are times when it's really quiet, and other times, extremely volatile. We have to feel its pulse before entering, else your account will be washed clean. There are three ways the market can move, an uptrend, a downtrend, and sideways. Look at the below images for an overview. You go long (i.e. buy) in an uptrend, you can go short (i.e. sell) in a downtrend, and when markets are in a sideways trend, I stop trading.

WHEN ASKED WHAT THE STOCK MARKET WILL DO: IT WILL FLUCTUATE.

- J.P MORGAN

Uptrending markets sit very well with my style, and during these market conditions, my objectives are achieved without much volatility to my equity curve. It's a nice zone to be in. We can identify if we are in these zones using some simple indicators I will discuss later in this chapter. Down trending markets are said to be very profitable also, but you need to be a really advanced trader before you trade these markets. And sideways markets can be really difficult to make money in if you don't have the right strategies to follow. In this book, I'm only going to cover up trending markets. It's so much fun.

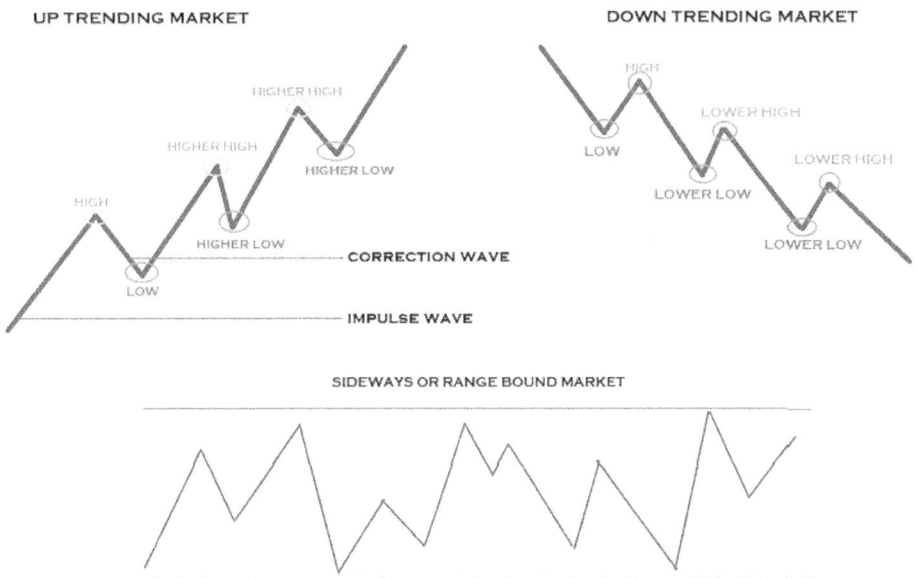

In an uptrending market, the price doesn't go up in a straight line, meaning it doesn't go up linearly. It goes up in a waveform. There are impulse waves and then correction waves. A wave having higher highs and higher lows is said to be an uptrending market. Do not take this definition literally; it's just an overview. There can be reversals anytime, so we always have to have our risk management in place. I look at the overall indices across the world to get an idea of how the markets are behaving with the current geopolitical news. For me, I try to match the news to the charts and try not to fit the charts to the news. It's because the charts have usually already been factored in the news. But there are always exceptions like Brexit in 2016 or scandals suddenly popping up in a company. It can literally be anything. The markets overreact a lot of the time; there will be sudden price swings. These are the times when a defensive position sizing strategy will save you from losing your capital overnight. There is an old Wall Street saying, "A trend is your friend until it ends."

We try to enter the uptrend after a correction wave, and again, when the price is back into an impulse wave. We do this to get the best entry point in terms of out Risk: Reward ratio. We will learn to trade with trend lines shortly. But different traders interpret these lines differently, so it's very subjective. By seeing these patterns, you will get an idea of where the price can go next. We use this in conjunction with other parameters to pinpoint stocks that have the highest probability to go up. In the American markets, there are over 7000 stocks, and the in the rest of the world combined there are over 50,000. And once we start filtering them using various strategies discussed below, we get to about 0-5 stocks a day. We have to be like a sniper, not wasting bullets; in our case, our capital. We have only 10 bullets (i.e. 10% risk). So I always have my risk management, take profit and stop loss in place to avoid all the unwanted drama in my head. These emotions can be like a little devil keeping you from making money.

1E. BUYERS AND SELLERS (OR) BULLS AND BEARS

> **ONE OF THE FUNNY THINGS ABOUT THE STOCK MARKET IS THAT EVERY TIME ONE PERSON BUYS, ANOTHER SELLS, AND BOTH THINK THEY ARE ASTUTE.**
>
> **-WILLIAM FEATHERS**

Buyers and sellers have the power to drive the price up or down. When buyers are taking control by buying more, the price goes up. And when the buyers are taking a rest or don't want to buy anymore, the sellers will take control driving the price down.

Imagine your account has $100,000 and you buy a stock. Don't expect it to go up. Your account is a small peanut compared to the other institutions. So don't ever expect to dictate the direction of a stock to go up or down. The only thing in you can do is proper analysis to narrow down stocks that have the highest probability to go up and control the size of your position. Stocks should be treated somewhat like your first date with someone. Don't invest too much in them, it could be a waste of time and money. Instead, spend time or money on them, if they have proved themselves, you can invest more.

1F. SUPPORT AND RESISTANCE

Support and resistance are areas in a chart where the price has a high probability of bouncing up or down. I base this analysis visually, using the moving averages, Trendlines or Fibonacci numbers.

You can research further about support and resistance concepts online. Below are some examples for your understanding.

1Fa. MOVING AVERAGES

One of the best ways to find out if the stock or stock indices are in an uptrend is by using a combination of moving averages. I use the following combinations to analyze the market.

1. The price has crossed above 50 EMA (Exponential Moving Average)
2. The 50 EMA has to be above the 100 EMA
3. The 100 EMA has to be above the 200 EMA

The chart should look something like this.

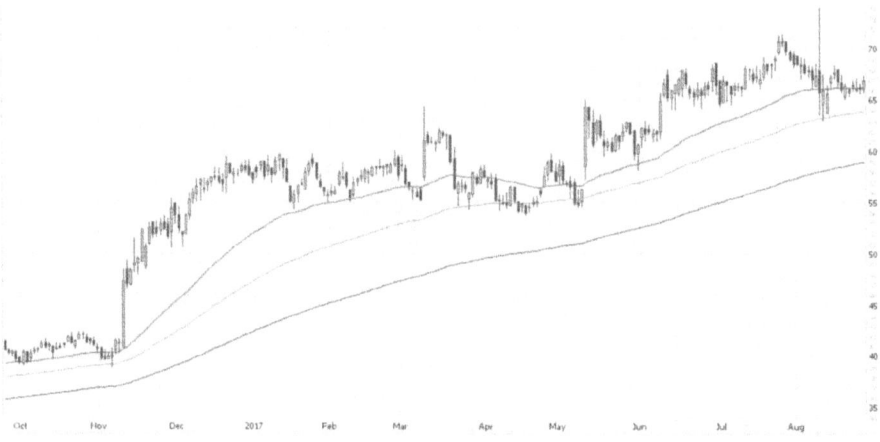

SOURCE: MARKETINOUT.COM

Beginners may find the entire concept of moving average difficult. Moving average is a commonly used lagging indicator. The input parameters are based on the strategy you are using. And an EMA or "Exponential moving average" is a type of moving average that is similar to a simple moving average (SMA), with more emphasis given to recent data. It is more responsive than an SMA. When you open the charts, try playing around with it, use different combinations to get the hang of it. The most commonly used ones are 8EMA, 21EMA, 50EMA, 100EMA, 150EMA, 200EMA, and 377EMA.

A moving average can be used in various strategies, and it also acts as a support and resistance line. Meaning the price usually finds it hard to break through these levels. The price usually rests on these lines before going up. This happens especially if it's strong numbers, such a 100 EMA, 150EMA, or 200EMA. These are really strong numbers, where most of the buying and selling happens. It's very important that we learn to respect Moving Averages. It also depends on the strategy you are using. In trading, everything is relative, so we cannot just use one indicator and jump straight into buying an asset.

When I was still a Rookie, I learned about moving average crossover strategy and thought it was the Holy Grail to making millions trading. So I traded using the following combinations. I was far from being right. But at the same time, I started losing less, and my equity curve slowly started looking toward growth.

This is the way I traded.

SHORT TERM STRATEGY: Buy when 6 EMA crossed 21 EMA

MEDIUM TERM STRATEGY: Buy when 16 EMA crossed 150 EMA

LONG-TERM STRATEGY: Buy when 21 EMA crossed 377 EMA.

This method was good, at least in the past, but this strategy uses lagging indicators. Placing a Stop Loss and a Take Profit based on my objectives was really difficult. And there was also literally no fundamental analysis to the stocks that I bought. This is a herd mentality, buying because everyone was buying, there will be so many stocks that meet this criteria on a day-to-day basis. So this strategy, by itself, doesn't fit my trading style. This was the strategy that really helped me get a feeling about trading stocks.

1Fb. TRENDLINES

A trendline can be drawn on any chart. The price movement of stocks can look really random to the naked eye. We have to try to break this down into patterns and zones. Trendlines are represented visually in any timeframe. A support line can become a resistance line and vice versa. If you don't yet understand, I hope you get it by looking at the pictures below. You can also do some research online for further knowledge.

Horizontal Trendlines that act as support and resistance

Sloping Support and Resistance Trendlines

In trading, you cannot be 100% certain about anything, the price can reverse and break through these lines. From my trading experience, I have learned that stocks respect these lines, at least most of the time. The best comparison I can give you is that of electricity when you switch the light on, and the bulb lights up. Can you see the current? It's the same way with these lines. Approach it with caution, and you can make money. But all lines will be broken at some point, and then the price will start to reverse. Trading using only support and resistance means that there are no fundamental analyses done on the stocks. So I had to go back to the drawing board, and I started looking for analysis that was both technical and fundamental. I had to narrow my search further to get an edge in the market.

BIG MONEY IS MADE IN THE STOCK MARKET BY BEING ON THE RIGHT SIDE OF THE MAJOR MOVES. THE IDEA IS TO GET IN HARMONY WITH THE MARKETS. IT'S SUICIDAL TO FIGHT TRENDS. THEY HAVE A HIGHER PROBABILITY OF CONTINUING THAN NOT.

MARTIN ZWEIG

Chapter 2

What's Your Edge; Do You Have Any?

In the previous chapter, we learned the business model of a casino. And, with a house edge of just 5.26%, they make millions every day or at least every month. This is exactly what we need to do. We need to develop an edge in the market that we can rely upon to make money consistently. Developing an edge takes a lot of time and effort, but only constitutes 20% of the overall success. However, if you don't spend the time, you will not make money consistently. I have put in 1,000s of hours of research to find strategies that fit my trading style. I am a swing trader, e.g. my trades last anywhere from a few days to a few months. I look for companies that have good fundamentals with strong momentum; I am not a value investor who is looking for cheap companies. I tried Day trading; it was not my cup of tea. Day trading is really fast, and I had other things to do, I didn't have the time to watch the price minute by minute. And longer term, years to decades, was really boring. Luckily for you, I am going to share the strategies I use, and the one that I have developed.

I follow a strict routine to scan for stocks; they should be of the highest quality and have the highest probability to go up in price. If it sounds complicated, don't worry. By the end of this chapter, I will explain each of these screeners and give you easy ways to detect them. Like driving a car or a bike, it's going to be a conscious effort that you have to put in. And then, once your conscious brain accepts these concepts, it will feed to your subconscious. So literally, it will become a task that takes about 20 minutes a day. The rest of the time you spend will be because of your interest in the markets. But this doesn't mean you start overtrading.

When you are buying a stock, you are basically buying a part of the business. So don't you want to know what you are buying, how well the business has done in the past, what is its growth potential, and are the technical signs showing a buy signal? You need to understand the reasons why a stock goes up, and it's definitely not random. Following these methods, really sit well with my trading style and fit logically in my head. So you can either choose to use my methods, or you can do the research and develop your own methods that fit you.

NO PRICE IS TOO LOW FOR A BEAR OR TOO HIGH FOR A BULL.

-STOCK MARKET PROVERB

2A. WILLIAM O'NIEL'S CANSLIM METHOD

Among many different strategies out there, I am a big fan of William O'Neil's CANSLIM. He is the founder of Investor's Business Daily (IBD). It is an American weekly newsletter covering stocks, ETF, mutual funds, etc. I really like this because the screening process for these stocks has a good level of reasoning behind it. But the main factor is the returns it has produced in the past. In the stock market, we can never predict what's coming, but that doesn't mean we can't use past performance.

According to AAII (American Association of Individual Investors), the results of the CANSLIM strategy are as follows.

Year-to-date	33.9%
3 Years	27.7%
5 Years	30%
10 years	15.4%

This sort of data proves that this method has worked in the past. So we will learn how to use this method for future results. But please be warned, past performance doesn't guarantee any future results that is why I use proper position sizing strategies to keep my risk under control along with our personal psychology.

2Aa. CANSLIM Acronym

C - Current quarterly earnings per share increased sharply from the same quarters' earnings reported in the prior year. This shows that the company has increased profit during the same quarter last year, and it should continue because the sales and profit have grown. Sometimes companies will discount goods, this will show an increase in sales, but the profit will have reduced.

A - Annual earnings for the stock should have increased over the past five years. The stock has to have proved itself for the last five years. So the odds that they will perform the same way are high.

N – There should be new products, new management, or new highs in price. Basically, the new factor will be a catalyst to drive the price higher.

S - Small supply and large demand for a stock create excess demand, it's an environment in which the price of the stock can go up drastically. When supply is lower than demand, the prices are bound to go up as there are more buyers than sellers. Companies acquiring their own stock reduce market supply and can indicate their expectation of future profitability. The companies should also have low debt-equity ratio.

L – Buy leading stocks instead of laggards within the same industry. A leader will go up faster and further than the laggards when the timing is good. Relative strength is used as a guide. Please note Relative strength (RS) is not the same as Relative Strength Index (RSI).

I - Pick stocks where there is institution buying. Institutions have big money, which could drive the price up. These institutions should be performing above average. Be cautious of stocks that are over-owned by institutions. They will not behave the same way.

M - Determining market direction by reviewing market averages daily. This can be done using simple moving average crossovers on the longer time frame, like weekly and monthly charts.

Don't worry if you don't completely understand the above. Using these filters correctly and to pick stocks can be really time-consuming, especially if you are new to the markets. Luckily,

William O'Neil is an entrepreneur who has created multiple businesses, among which, Market Smith (MS) is one of them. This software screens for stocks with various pre-set filters and delivers notification as and when they come. There are various subscription options available. It is also available on the Apple's App Store. But do not subscribe on the app store, there are some features that are missing, such as pattern recognition. Use only the trial version on the Apple's app store to get a feel for the App. Then when you decide to subscribe, go directly to https://marketsmith.investors.com/.

As I said earlier, the analysis we do can be done for any stock across the globe, and MS is available for U.S, Hong Kong, and Indian Stocks. So you receive notifications for about 20 hours a day across the different markets. Have you heard the phrase, "Money never sleeps?" Maybe this is why. There are pre-set screening filters in MS, and one of them is growth 250, breaking out today. I use this day in day out. Apart from this, there are many different pre-set filters. Get the trial version and explore. It is one of the best products out there for stock selection. The stocks that are notified have really good risk-reward ratios, and the software itself shows the Stop Loss and Take Profit zones, making it an essential for a swing trader's toolkit.

Some of the stocks that MS has sent notifications in the past are as below. This is just a basic chart of the stock that I am showing you from marketinout.com. However, Market Smith has a lot more details on their charts. So I would advise getting the free or the 3-week trial they offer and experience it first-hand.

1. OSUR – Orasure Technologies

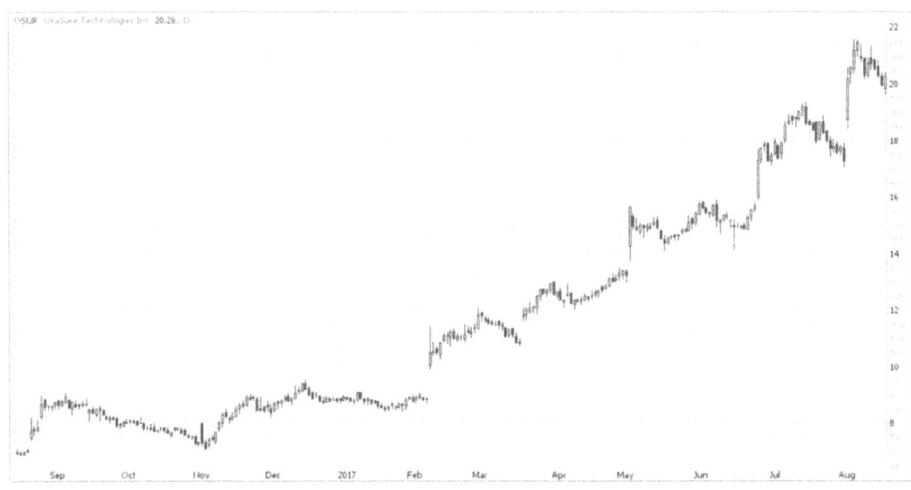

SOURCE: MARKETINOUT.COM

2. PETS – Petmed Express

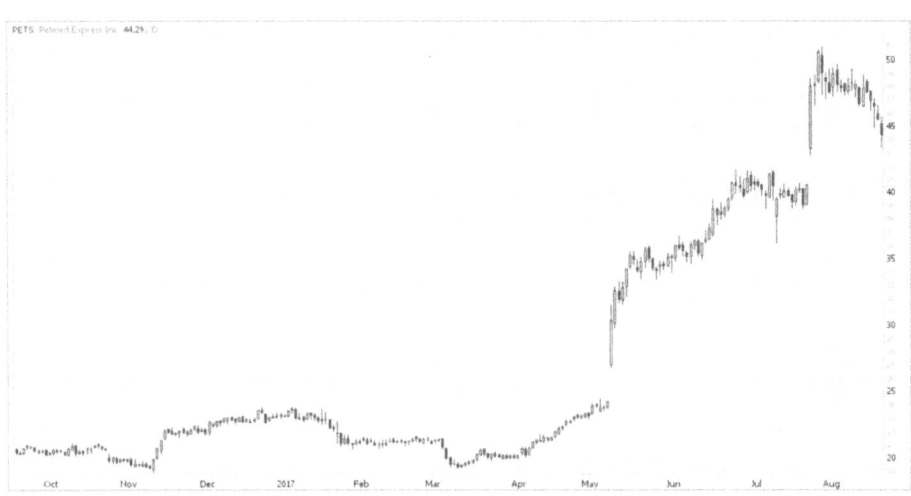

SOURCE: MARKETINOUT.COM

3. BZUN – Baozun

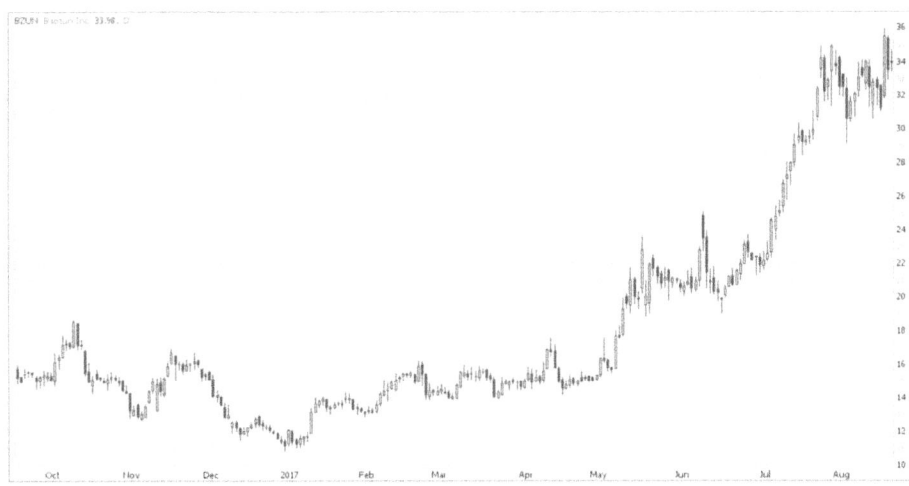

SOURCE: MARKETINOUT.COM

4. ATHM – Autohome

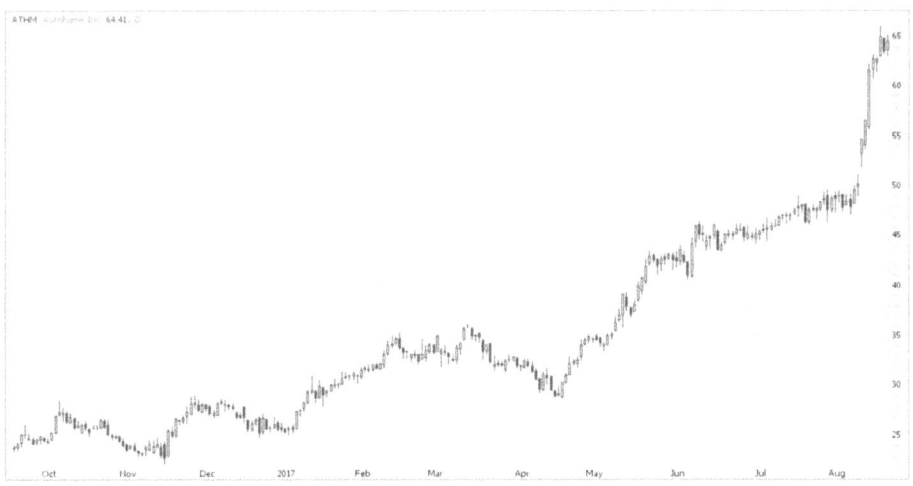

SOURCE: MARKETINOUT.COM

5. EXAS – Exact Sciences Corp

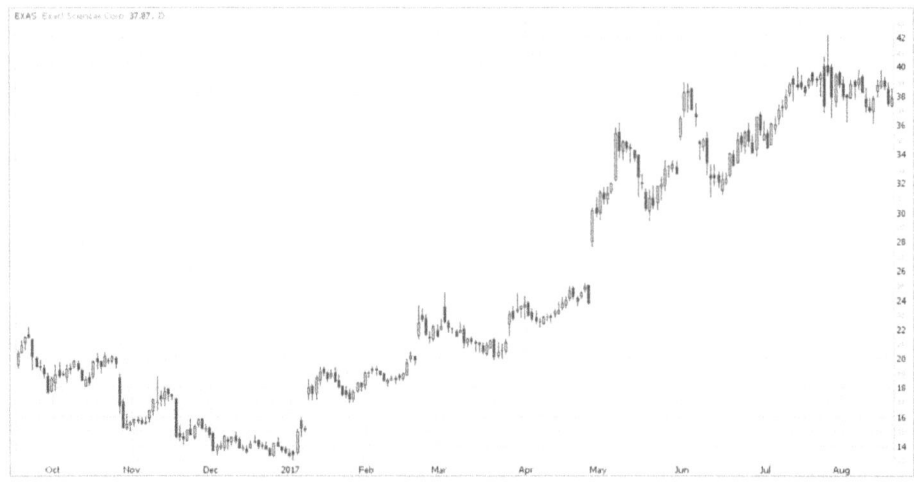

SOURCE: MARKETINOUT.COM

6. ROG – Rogers Corp

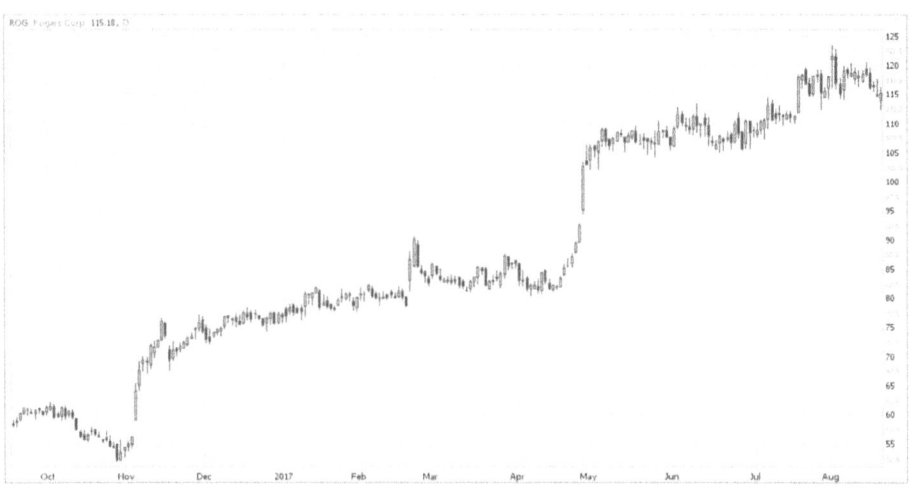

SOURCE: MARKETINOUT.COM

7. YY – YY Inc

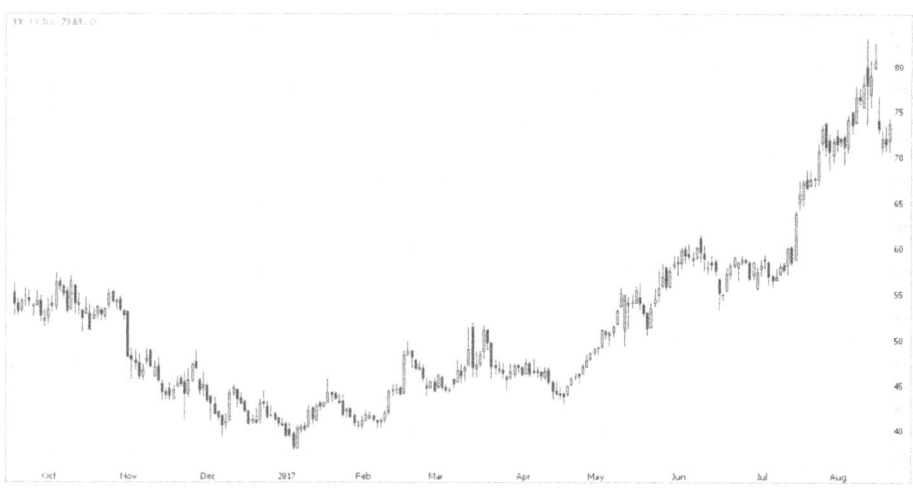

SOURCE: MARKETINOUT.COM

8. NVDA – NVIDIA Corp

SOURCE: MARKETINOUT.COM

9. JKS – Jinko Solar Holdings

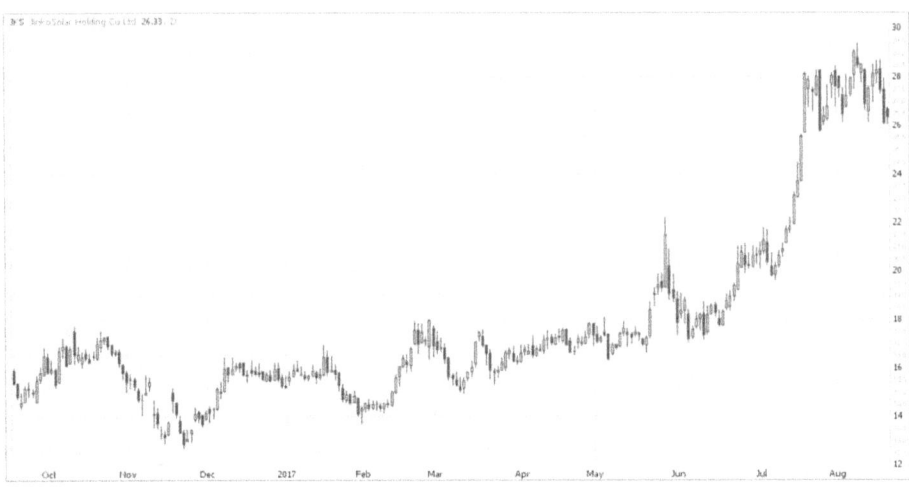

SOURCE: MARKETINOUT.COM

10. WTW – Weight Watchers International

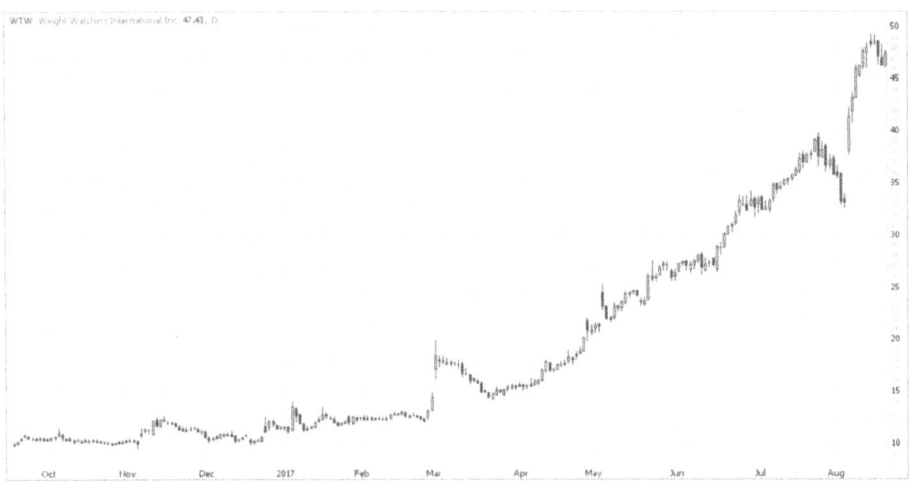

SOURCE: MARKETINOUT.COM

As you can see from the above charts, you would have made a lot of money trading using this system. However, don't immediately think you will be a millionaire overnight trading this system. I have shown you only the winning trades. Like all trading systems, there will be losing trades as well. That is why position sizing is so important. This system produces more winners than losers over time, and I ride the winners for a long time. Sometimes I even have 10R profit targets, so the money I make from 1 stock will be enough to cover 10 losing trades.

Even though the results produced by this system are exceptional over time, I do not risk more than 1% on any given trade. Since my objective for cumulative risk is 10R or 10%, it doesn't mean that I only have 10 open positions. Sometimes, the number of open positions will be more than 10, even 20. This way, I control my downside and open the potential for the upside more than 30R. I do this with position sizing strategies that you will learn in the next chapter.

2B. SCREENING FOR STOCKS

I want to buy stocks that have good fundamental and technical analysis (FUNTECH). It is impossible to screen for stocks manually using my set criteria. There are thousands of stocks that have to be analyzed. So I use MARKETINOUT.COM to screen for these stocks. MARKETINOUT.COM has some really good filters, and they fit very well with my trading style. From my memory, you can scan up to 3 times a day for free on MARKETINOUT.COM, and then you have to subscribe. I have spent 100's of hours putting these filters together. I am going to share these with you. I will explain each of the filters, and how a combination of these filters will narrow the search from 1,000s of stocks to between 0 - 5 a day. Some days there will be no stocks that meet my criteria, so don't trade those days. It's really straightforward, go to MARKETINOUT.COM and select stock screener under the trader's tools tab, and then input the below criteria to get the results. An additional filter for the exchange you are trading in can also be added. My screeners will not have them, as I am going to show you only U.S shares.

MARKETINOUT.COM

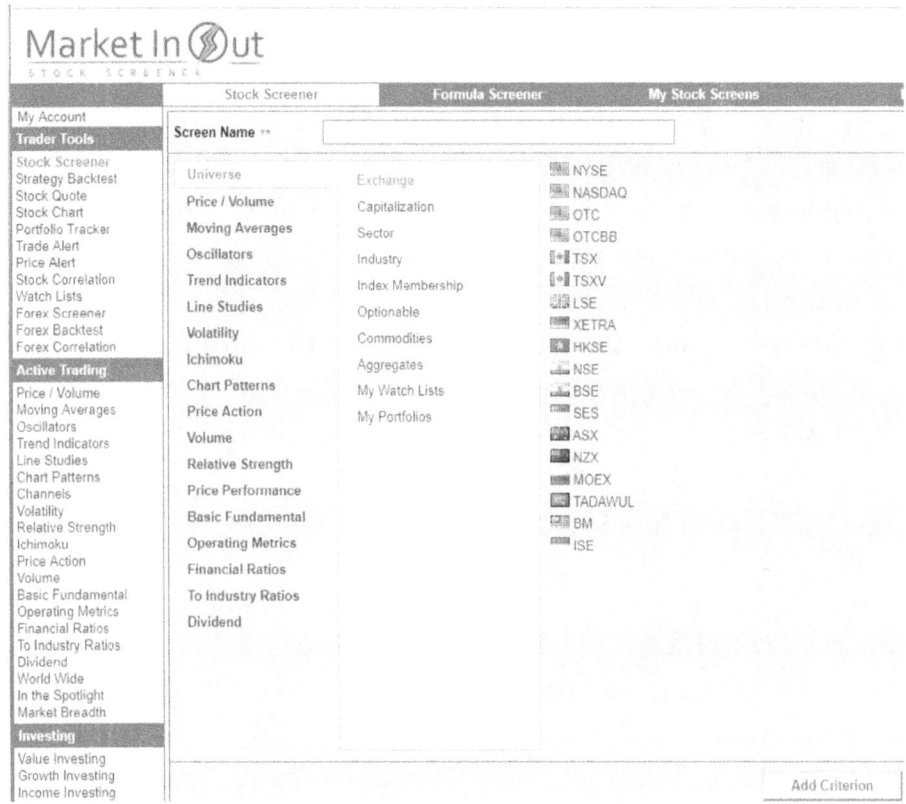

I will show you three of my screeners, each of them will have seven filters. The first six of these filters will be common to all, but there will be one filter that will be changing based on the strategy. Make sure you read each of the below filters and input them correctly in MARKETINOUT.COM.

2Ba. KARTHIK'S BRT

1. EMA (50) is above EMA (100)

2. EMA (100) is above EMA (200)

When applied, these above two filters will show the stocks that are in a clear uptrend.

3. AVERAGE VOLUME is greater than 0.1 million

This filter will show stocks that are liquid. Stocks need to be liquid so that it is easy to get in and out. This reduces the buy/sell or spread price.

4. EPS to industry greater than 200%

In any stock, the EPS or Earning Per share is an extremely important indicator that shows the profitability of the company. You can read more about this online. This filter shows companies that have an EPS that is 200 times the industry average; we want stocks that are leaders in EPS.

5. EPS, 5-year growth is greater than 10%

We know that a company's EPS is extremely important, and a company that shows a 10% growth in EPS for the past 5 years is an excellent stock to buy. It has been proving itself over and over again.

6. Profit margin to industry is greater than 200%

I like companies that have really high profits. A company that has 200 times the profit of the industry it's in. This tells me they have enough capital for deployment into new products and markets.

7. Bounced up from Rising Trendline

We have learned earlier that an upward sloping support trendline offers good low-risk entry points. There can be 100s of companies with good fundamentals. We also need to have a good technical signal to buy a stock. This is one of my best strategies; it gives me exactly what I want. It's a very selective combination of filters that I use, so there are only a few companies that meet all these criteria. And I am willing to bet on them. Only for this screening criterion, I place a Stop just below the trendline to get better Risk: Reward ratio.

Stocks that showed up with this criterion.

1. ALGN: Align Technology Inc

SOURCE: MARKETINOUT.COM

2. CACC: Credit Acceptance Corp

SOURCE: MARKETINOUT.COM

3. EFX: Equifax Inc

SOURCE: MARKETINOUT.COM

4. Monolithic Power Systems Inc

SOURCE: MARKETINOUT.COM

5. NOC: Northrop Grumman Corp

SOURCE: MARKETINOUT.COM

2Bb. KARTHIK'S CRT

1. EMA (50) is above EMA (100)

2. EMA (100) is above EMA (200)

These above two filters will show the stocks that are in a clear uptrend.

3. AVERAGE VOLUME is greater than 0.1 million

This filter will show stocks that are liquid; stocks have to be liquid so that it is easy to get in and out. This reduces the buy/sell price or spread price.

4. EPS to industry greater than 200%

In any stock, the EPS or Earning Per share is an extremely important indicator that shows the profitability of the company. You can read more about this online. This filter shows companies that have an EPS that is 200 times the industry average; we want stocks that are leaders in EPS.

5. EPS, 5-year growth is greater than 10%

We know that the companies EPS is extremely important, and a company that shows a 10% growth year on year with respect to EPS is an excellent company to buy. It has been proving itself over and over again.

6. Profit margin to industry is greater than 200%

I like companies that have really high profits. A company that has 200 times the profit of the industry tells me they have enough capital for deployment into new products and markets.

7. Crossed above Rising Trendline (CRT)

When a stock with such good fundamentals crosses above the rising trend line, it enters a new zone where the previous resistances become support, and there is no headwind or resistance in the near future. When this is the case, the potential for the stock to go up is really high.

I like to think that Technical analysis shows me the direction and timing, and then fundamental analysis acts as the fuel to propel the stock to greater heights.

Some stocks that have shown up using this screen are below.

1. **ATHM – Autohome Inc**

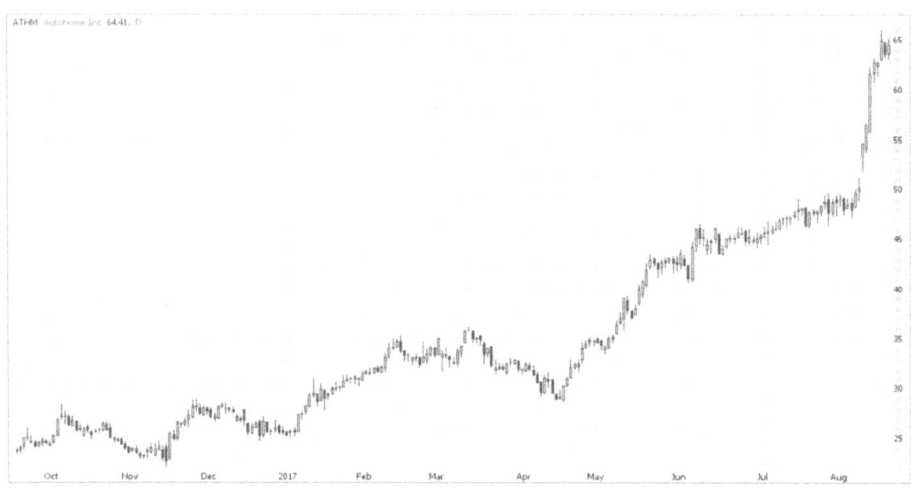

SOURCE: MARKETINOUT.COM

2. ALGN – Align Technology

SOURCE: MARKETINOUT.COM

3. GRUB – Grubhub Inc

SOURCE: MARKETINOUT.COM

4. LMT- Lockheed Martin Corp

SOURCE: MARKETINOUT.COM

2Bc. KARTHIK'S FIBONACCI RETRACEMENT

The Fibonacci numbers are a sequence of numbers developed by an Italian mathematician, Leonardo Pisano. The sequence goes like this... 0, 1, 1, 2, 3, 5, 8, 13, 21, 34 ... The next number is found by adding up the two numbers before it. So the next number will be 21+34 = 55 then it will be 34+55 = 89 and so on.

They appear everywhere in Nature, from the leaf arrangement in plants to the pattern of the florets of a flower, from the bracts of a pinecone to the scales of a pineapple. The Fibonacci numbers are therefore applicable to the growth of every living thing, including a single cell, a grain of wheat, a hive of bees, and even all of mankind. Like everywhere in nature, they are also found in the stock market. I am not here to argue why it occurs. They just do, so I use them to find stocks. Remember, we learned that in an uptrend, the stock goes up in a wave pattern. An impulse wave, which is then followed by a correction wave. The correction wave can also retrace back to a Fibonacci number: The key Fibonacci ratios of 23.6%, 38.2%, 61.8%, and then there is also 50% retracement. Though 50% is not a Fibonacci number, we still use it, since a bouncing up after a 50% retracement with strong fundamentals has the potential to go up. But I screen only with 0.62% since it represents a good pullback.

SCREENING CRITERIA

1. EMA (50) is above EMA (100)
2. EMA (100) is above EMA (200)

These above two filters will filter and show the stocks that are in a clear uptrend.

3. AVERAGE VOLUME is greater than 0.1 million

This filter will show stocks that are liquid; stocks have to be liquid so that it is easy to get in and out. This reduces the buy/sell price or spread price.

4. EPS to industry greater than 200%

In any stock, the EPS or Earning Per share is an extremely important indicator that shows the profitability of the company. You can read more about this online. This filter shows companies that have an EPS that is 200 times the industry average; we want stocks that are leaders in EPS.

5. EPS, 5-year growth is greater than 10%

We know that the companies EPS is extremely important, and a company that shows a 10% growth year on year with respect to EPS is an excellent company to buy. It has been proving itself over and over again.

6. Profit margin to industry is greater than 200%

I like companies that have really high profits. A company that has 200 times the profit of the industry tells me they have enough capital for deployment into new products and markets.

7. Bounced up from Fibo 0.62

What this means, is that the price has touched or retraced to the 0.62 level and then bounced back into the uptrend, it represents a new impulse wave. It provides a low-risk entry point with good reward potential.

Some stocks that have come up in the past few months are

1. **WGO – Winnebago**

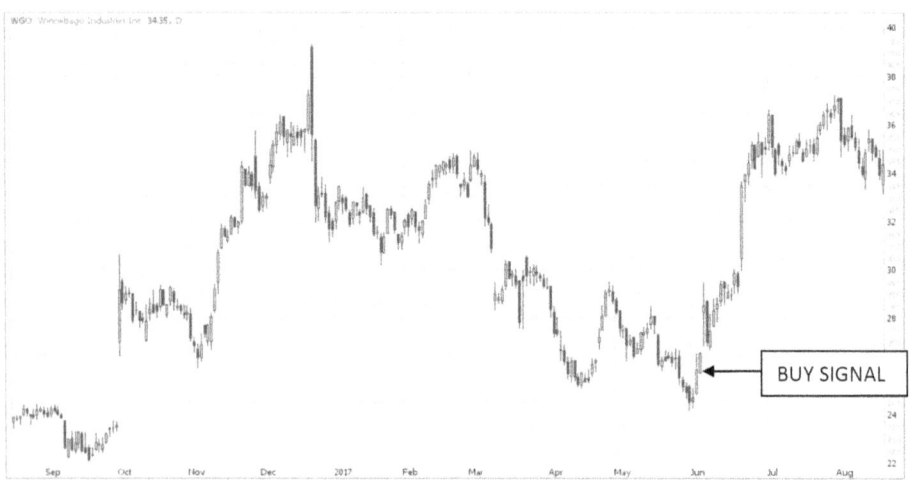

SOURCE: MARKETINOUT.COM

For all the three strategies that are mentioned, you can either choose daily or weekly charts based on your preference. Some days there will be no trades at all. Relax and do some research or watch something online. These are times when you will want to over trade and break your rules, so this is something to watch out for. If no stocks are showing up for a few days to a few weeks, note that you now entering a Bear market.

The above strategies are for an up-trending bull market, they will not work during a Bear market. I have not seen any strategies that work well in both Bear and bull markets. You have to be flexible to change your strategy based on the market you are trading. A simple way to determine this is using combinations of moving averages, which I have shown you earlier. And there is a lot of money to be made in Bear markets as well, but I am covering only strategies that you can use in bull markets

In this chapter, I have shown you four methods or strategies that I use on a day-to-day basis to find stocks. This method is for U.S equities; you can add an additional filter, EXCHANGE, to screen for stocks in the markets you are trading. Market Smith is available in 3 countries; the U.S, Hong Kong, and India.

We have crossed the 20% mark required to be a successfully profitable trader. Many people just learn the strategies and think they will make money consistently. They are far from being right. 80% of success comes from correct position sizing and personal psychology. Without either of these, you will never make money consistently, unless short-term luck gives you a hand. And luck is something that easily runs out in the markets. So make sure you understand the next two chapters before you dive into buying stocks.

Chapter 3

Position Sizing

EVERYONE HAS THE BRAINPOWER TO FOLLOW THE STOCK MARKET. IF YOU MADE IT THROUGH FIFTH GRADE MATH, YOU CAN DO IT.

-PETER LYNCH

According to me, a good position sizing strategy will give you an edge in markets. The concept of position sizing was developed by Dr. Van Tharp. He was featured in the 1st Market Wizards book. He says that the greatest secret in trading and investing is the application of proper position sizing. Your success depends on how much you invest in a particular stock or any asset. According to him, size does matter in the markets.

There is a game that to help you understand, it goes something like this. If a bag contains 100 balls, 50 are red and 50 are green. The green represents a winning trade, and a red ball represents a losing trade. So, from this, there is a 50:50 chance of getting a winning trade or losing trade. The order of how these balls appear is random. When this experiment is done among a group of people, the results vary drastically. Note that the order of the winning and losing trades can be the same for all the people, but they allocate their trading capital (different position size) differently based on their own logic, greed, and fear. Some are really greedy, so they invest more, and some are really fearful, so they invest less. The variation in the results can be up to 90% at the end of the game. Even though the order of trades was the same for all the players, at the end of the game, some have gone bankrupt, and some have become millionaires. The only variable was their position sizing strategy. This is when you realize that mathematics wins over luck in a game of chance. A successful trader will have the same or, in some cases, more losing trades. They can have a higher number of losing trades, where they lose little, and have a lower percentage of winning trades where they make much more than their losing trades combined. At the end of the day, they are successful because they cut their losses at planned intervals and let the winning trades reach their full potential.

What I want from a position sizing strategy is; I want small controlled drawdown, and I want the maximum profit potential. When you have an edge in the market, you will have more winners, or your winners will be much bigger than your losers, and from correct position sizing strategy, you can achieve your objectives. Dr. Van Tharp's book "Definitive guide to position sizing" has over 90 different models to choose from. He shares the ones that he likes and dislikes. There are some really dangerous models, such as the Martingale Model. When I was a rookie trader, I tried the Martingale Method, and I lost a lot of money. I have managed to take the ones that best suit my trading style and risk tolerance, and use them in my trading. Only when I started to apply correct position sizing strategy for my trades, was I able to meet my objectives. The use of proper position sizing strategies contributes to 30% of your overall success. After learning the methods I use, you will have the crossed 50% mark required to be a consistently profitable trader. After reading this chapter, you will be able to understand how a pro uses position sizing to make money consistently.

3A. RISKING A PERCENTAGE OF YOUR TOTAL EQUITY

> ### "RULE #1: NEVER LOSE MONEY; RULE #2: NEVER FORGET RULE #1"
>
> ### -WARREN BUFFET

Controlling risk should be your top priority as a trader. If you lose your capital, you cannot trade. Losing a significant portion of your capital on any single trade can affect your emotions, which in turn, will affect your performance as a trader. When you are constantly checking your account balance every minute, note that it's a sign that you are risking more than what you can digest. The first years of my trading were exactly like this, I would risk too much, I would have small profits and close my positions, and the same time, really big losses. In some cases, I lost up to 50% of my equity on a single position. I never had a trading journal. I basically possessed all the qualities of a Rookie trader.

So for a newbie, I recommend risking about 0.25% to 0.50% of your capital. If you have capital below $10,000, you should rethink trading. It is possible with low capital, but it will be difficult. So I recommend starting with a capital of $10,000 or its equivalent in the country you are trading. Once you get a feel for the markets, then you can risk a maximum of 1%. That's the maximum I will go up to. I get notifications every day, I need to be capitalized to deploy my capital to buy these stocks. Rather than buying a big chunk of a single stock, I like to take smaller bites. It will be easy for your inner child to handle. There is no single stock that you buy that will make you a millionaire overnight. If you lose a big chunk of your equity, you will give up trading faster because you will keep losing money and get depressed. This is a state that you don't want to be in.

If my total equity is $10,000, what does 1% risk mean? I.e. $100 risk (1% of $10,000 = $100)

Position 1: If a stock is trading at $20, does this mean I buy only 5 shares? You may think $20 a share * 5 shares =$100. No, without knowing when I will exit, either if I'm right or if I'm wrong, I will never enter the trade.

Suppose I want to get out when the price of the stock drops to $18 (a 10% drop from the opening price). This means I am willing to risk $2 per share.

Initial risk: $100
Risk per share: $2
Number of share to buy = Initial risk/ risk per share
      = 100/ 2
      = 50 shares

So I can buy 50 shares costing $20 each = $1,000. Even though my total investment is $1,000, the maximum I can lose is $100. Because I know when I will get out when it's gone wrong. It is essential you learn this and start applying it to your trades. Have planned and controlled risk. Don't let any of your positions surprise you.

Position 2: If a stock is at $50 and my initial risk is 1% or $100 (1% of $10,000), and my stop loss is at $40. How many shares can I buy?

Initial risk: $100
Risk per share: $10 ($50 - $40)
Number of shares I can buy = 100/10
= 10 shares

The investment for this stock is $500 ($50 per share * 10 shares), but the risk is only $100. I hope you can start making sense from the above 2 examples. If not, read them again. It's important that you understand this before going ahead.

Position 3: If a stock is at $100 and I decide to get out at $85. Let's look at the calculation below.

Initial risk: $100
Risk per share: $ 15 ($100 - $85)
Number of shares to buy = 100/15
= 6.6 or 6 shares

The investment for this position is $600 ($100 per share* 6 shares), but the risk is only $100.

From the above examples, we can now calculate the cumulative risk of all our positions. We have 3 positions and the total value of my investment is $1000 + $500 + $600 =$2,100. The total investment may be $2,100, but the maximum I can lose if these three positions go against me is $300 ($100 in each position * 3). So we can now say that the cumulative risk is 3% of my portfolio of $10,000.

So far, I have shown you what I buy, and how much I buy based on my 1% risk rule. I do this until I have a maximum of 10R or 10% risk. So if my equity is $10,000, the maximum I could lose if all the 10 positions go against me is $1,000.

3B. THINK 'R' MULTIPLES

Here 'R' stands for Risk and Reward. In my trading business, my initial risk is 1%, i.e. 1R = 1%. You should always calculate your 'R' before entering a trade. Looking at my trading journal, my R multiples are always in the range of 0.95R to 1.15R. It's difficult to have exactly 1R, but that should be what the baseline is. I have a strict 'R' discipline. Thinking in terms of 'R' multiples should be engraved into your DNA as a trader, only then, will your confidence and performance increase. I set my target profit to 3R or more. What this means is that I will win 3 times my initial risk. So this makes my Risk: Reward ratio 1: 3. Can you do the basic math and see that I make money even if I am only right 50% of the time?

Example: **If a stock is trading at $25. My stop loss is at $22. I place my take profit at $35. If I have $10,000 equity, I am willing to risk 1% or $100. I can buy about 33 (100/3) shares. If this position goes against me, I lose $100. And if I win I make $330. Here 1R = $3, So when I lose, I lose $3 a share and when I win I win $10 a share. Can you start making sense of what 'R' is and how you should have bigger wins and smaller losses?**

3C. CALCULATING EXPECTANCY

We always have to calculate expectancy in our trading business. We gather the data to see if we are making profit or loss trading a particular system. Calculating expectancy is fairly simple.

The formula to calculate expectancy is = [(winning percentage * Average win) – (Losing percentage * Average loss)]/ average amount risked

In my trading account, suppose I have $10,000, and I have 50% wins and 50% losses. And suppose I make $300 on my wins, and I lose $100 on my losing trades. My expectancy is as follows.

= [(50%*300) – (50%*100)]/$100
=[150-$50]/100
= $100/$100
=$1

So what this means, is that for every dollar I risk, I make one dollar.

So I have risked $100 per trade * 100 trades = $10,000. Based on this system, I make $1 for every $1 I risk. So in a total of 100 trades, I risk $10,000 (100*$100) to make $10,000. So at the end of 100 trades, my account balance will be $20,000. This means I am able to double my money every 100 trades. To get this sort of return, you should always hunt for the top-quality stocks and follow correct position sizing strategy. And always have a maximum of 10% cumulative risk. Remember, slow and steady makes you money.

Suppose a rookie trader has $10,000 and they just want to be right, rather than to make money, it will look something like this: In 100 trades, they can be right 70% of the time, because they will only take $100 profits, and 30% of the time, they will be wrong and they will have $500 losses. They are hoping for their losing trades to become profitable. This rarely happens.

= [(winning % * Average win) – (Losing % * Average loss)]/ average risk amount

Here, average risk amount is [(70 trades*100 avg win) + (30 trades*500 avg loss)]/100 trades = $220

= [(70%*100) − (30%*500)]/$220
= ($70-$150)/$220
= -$0.36

So what they have is a negative expectancy. This means that for every $1 they bet, they lose 0.36 cents. So for a rookie trader starting with $10,000, they will lose $3,600. After 100 trades, their account balance will be $6,400. This is by wanting to be right rather than to make more money when they are right and lose less when they are wrong. They will not be profitable in the business of trading.

If you are a new trader, you will not be able to calculate expectancy because you do not have enough data. Once you set the rules and have completed about 50 trades, you should be able to calculate your expectancy. If you know what it is based on your previous trades, you will then be able to forecast what you can expect from your trading system in the future. If you have a positive expectancy, you can carry on trading the same way. On the other hand, if you have a negative expectancy, you should stop trading and rework your strategy or position sizing strategy. I hope you are now able to start thinking in terms of 'R' multiples and expectancy.

3D. STOPLOSS & TAKEPROFIT

As I have mentioned earlier, if you want to be a pro, you have to have a STOPLOSS (SL) order and TAKEPROFIT (TP) order for each of your trades. If you don't, I consider you a gambler, not a trader, and you will never be able to make consistent money trading. I always have an SL and TP order to control my risk at any given time. And unlike a casino, trading can yield losses that are more than your deposit, so be careful in choosing your trading vehicle. Leveraged products can be really dangerous for novice trader, so make sure to enter a trade with SL and TP orders. One of the main advantages of SL and TP orders is its like automatic pruning. Your bad decisions are cut short, and your good decisions are left to run. This is essentially what you want. I know I have been emphasizing a lot on SL and TP orders. I have faced really bad periods during my course of trading. At those times, I wished I had placed SL and TP orders.

Having too tight an SL will get you out of positions that you were supposed to be in. In trading, we call this Whipsawed. I have an SL of about 5% – 7% of the stock price. 5%- 7% of the stock price will equate to my initial 1R risk. I hope you are able to relate both of them. Having a 5%- 7% SL on your position doesn't mean you have a 5R -7R risk to your portfolio. You can have as big an SL as you want, but that should equate only to a maximum of 1R risk to your portfolio. For my TP orders, I set them at 3R or more, depending on each trade. I have nothing below 2.5R TP.

Example: A stock is trading at $15. Based on the previous low, I place my SL order at $13.50 (also 10% below my opening price). So where do I place my TP?

My objective is to gain 3 times what I lose. So I could lose $1.50 per share which is 1R. So if I want a 3R gain. I just multiple $1.5*3= $4.50. Now I add the opening price to $4.50 = $19.50. This is where I place my TP order. I may up it by a few cents to $20.00 so that my commission and spread are also factored in. That means that NETT, I make sure I have a 3R gain. Once you follow this simple rule to keep your winning trades 3 times your losing trades, you are bound to make money, provided your strategy works during these market periods.

3E. BREAKEVEN & FREE MONEY

This is a bit advanced for new traders, so read it slowly and carefully. Once my trade starts moving up into the profit zone, reaching about 2R in profit, I immediately move my SL to the opening price or just a few cents higher. I do this so that if the stock turns around and starts to drop in price, then I get out with no loss, or I breakeven for that position. This is the primary reason why I do this. The other reason is that I will have freed up my capital that I initially allocated. Meaning once I move my SL to the opening price, I still have the 10R TP with a 0R risk. Remember, this is what we call 'FREE money' i.e. you are risking only the money that the market is giving you. You can also use this strategy to open multiple positions in the same stock without having a risk of more than 1R.

Example:

1st position 1R SL: 10R TP,
2nd position 1R SL: 6R TP, (by now your 1st position would have 0R risk, since your initial SL is higher than your open price)
3rd position 1R SL: 3R RP, (by now your 2nd position would also have a 0R risk, since you moved your 2nd SL also to higher than the open price)

So a combined risk of just 1R (i.e. only 3rd position has a 1R risk, 1st and 2nd positions now have 0R risk) with a profit potential of 10R + 6R + 3R= 19R, this means you are risking 1% to make 19%. Wouldn't you like that? Not everyone gets lucky with these kinds of trades, but it is definitely possible. And make sure for each stock you have a maximum of 3 open positions with a combined risk of just 1R. If you are a beginner, I would recommend to just using the breakeven part of this strategy, and don't use the free money without a proper buy signal. If you get a buy signal after you have moved the 1st positions' SL to higher than the open price, which makes this trade a no loss trade, only then, would I recommend opening the 2nd position. Don't just open one because the stock went up a few cents.

In this chapter we learnt that it is essential know when to get out of the stock if you are right or wrong. Based on this we know how much to invest in a particular stock. So we now know "**What**" and "**When to buy**" based our strategy, we know "**When to sell**" and "**How much to Buy**" of a particular stock based on our Position Sizing. We have crossed the 50% mark required to be a successfully profitable trader.

Chapter 4

Psychology and Emotions

Trading is a business that comes with a lot of emotional baggage. In England, you will sometimes experience all four weather seasons in the same day. Similarly, when you are trading, you will face emotions like Greed, Fear, Hope, Excitement, Anger, etc. all at the same time. All traders face this, but only pros keep them under control. Even if they have these emotions, it won't affect their performance. Your own psychology contributes to 50% of your overall success, so it is essential you read and understand this chapter clearly. It's really not difficult; I have actually given you subtle details in the previous chapters that will enable you to keep your emotions in check. Let's look at each of the situations you will be facing and how it can be avoided.

STOCK MARKET BUBBLES DON'T GROW OUT OF THIN AIR. THEY HAVE SOLID BASIS IN REALITY, BUT REALITY IS DISTORTED BY MISCONCEPTION.

-GEORGE SOROS

CYCLE OF MARKET EMOTIONS

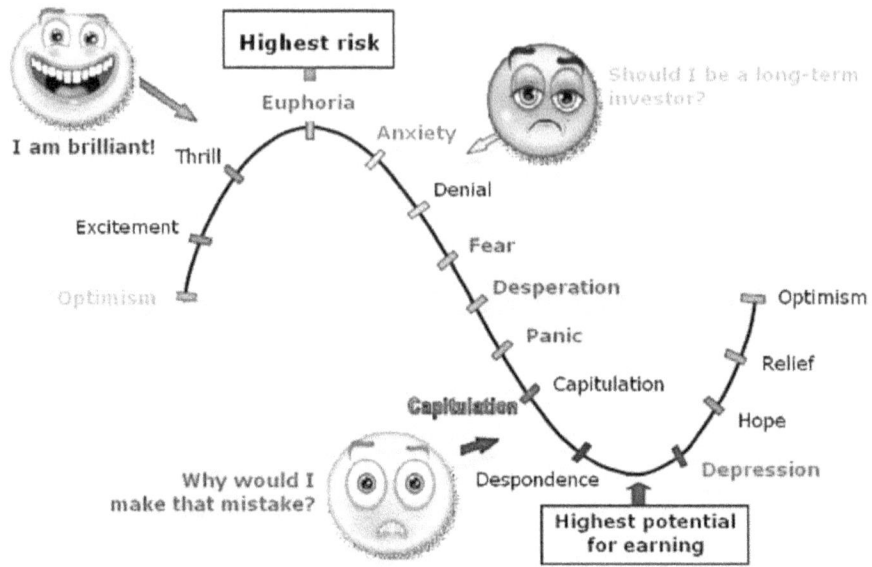

SOURCE: GOOGLE.COM

The above chart explains the price movement of a stock, or any asset for that matter. Let us go through each of the emotions.

Optimism: So you have spent 100s hours learning how to pick stocks, then you are certain that the stock will go up. So you place a big bet, more than you think you can handle. You have got the stock correct, the price starts moving up. You feel optimistic about the stock.

Excitement: The stock has started to move in your favor, and your account starts showing some small profits. You are now excited, the thought of being a millionaire flashes in your head. You think you are now the smartest money manager the world has ever seen.

Thrill: The price goes up even more. You are thrilled about your investment, you start jumping around. You start making plans for all the money you are about to make. You start telling your friends about the possibilities in the market. You are now celebrating, thinking about your potential profit.

Euphoria: You see the news and the stock you picked is just flashing green. You are now on top of the world. If you didn't invest all your money the first time, now you are thinking the stock will go through the roof, so you want to invest even more.

Anxiety: The price starts to dip by a few cents. This emotion is now triggered. You are now on your computer screen, seeing the price move every tick. Since you have got a good company stock, you start to think and want to believe that your trade is now a long-term investment.

Denial: The price starts to go down further by a few cents. Now you are looking at your analysis again and again. There seems to be nothing wrong. It's fundamentally a strong company; you got in when the technical sign gave you a buy signal. At this stage, you are still in profit by a few cents. But you are denying the fact that this downtrend could happen. The question that arises is, "how is it even possible for the price to go down?"

Fear: Now the price is almost at the opening level. You are still just a few cents in profit, just enough to show that you made a profit and covered the commissions. Some people can't be wrong, they hate to be wrong. So they take the small profit and console themselves saying, "at least I didn't lose money, or I just have a breakeven position."

Desperation: Your position has started to turn red. You are slowly starting to lose your money. You are now desperate for the stock to move back up. You miss your meal, staring at the screen, wanting the price to go back up. You wish you had at least got out when there was a small profit.

Panic: The money you invested might not have been meant for trading, or you borrowed it. Now you're trying to find all the answers to the questions your wife, husband, or whoever are going to ask you. This is a bad state to be in. The market is slowly turning you into a liar.

Capitulation: Now there is panic selling taking place in the stock. You can't take it anymore. Your account has a 50% or more decline. You are thinking, "if I have the position open for longer, I will lose the rest of the money." So you close the position at a loss. You are thinking about how long you have to work to make up all this lost money.

Despondence: You have closed your position, and now with a huge 50% drawdown, you think that you will never be a successful trader. Thoughts like; Trading is just gambling, it should be avoided at all costs. Actually, this is the time where the pros start looking at the stock. Some professional traders say that they only buy when there is 'blood on the street,' meaning everyone is really pessimistic and wants to get out of the stock. So they are selling at whatever price they can. Value investors start their hunt to pick stocks that are in this state.

Depression: Now the depression cocktail floods your brain. This is when the pros start buying the asset. The pros and institutions usually have big money. The number of players can be less, but their trade size can be really big. So the buyers are now taking control of the stock. The price slowly starts going up. You are now feeling bad; you are wishing that you should have kept the position open. The pros only buy the best of assets at the lowest possible price. And they do not allow any one position to make them feel these roller coasters of emotions. You want to be in this state to make money consistently.

Hope: For the traders who still haven't closed their position, a sense of hope rushes through them. Now they are sitting tight with their position, hoping for the stock price to go up so that they can get out, or at least break even.

Relief: The price of the stock is back to the initial opening price. Now a big sense of relief is there. You are now up, and your position slowly starts turning around making your position green. It puts a sense of relief through your head.

And then the cycle repeats itself. You faced all this drama in your head because you invested more than you could digest. Think and analyze what you can digest? Can you just digest a 0.5% loss, or can you digest a 50% loss? It's up to you. Can you live happily if you lost the money, or is it money that you could afford to lose? As a professional trader, you should always be capitalized to take advantage of situations when they arise. So investing more on any given stock is not their objective. They don't want to experience all this drama, they think of it as business. They don't want to allocate more than 1% of their resources. Even profitable hedge funds, who manage billions, have strict rules. Some of them don't risk more than 0.5% of their portfolio on any given stock.

Let's look at some of these emotions in detail.

SITUATION 1: GREED

Once you have done your research on a particular stock, based the strategies that I have shown above or because you got a notification from the guru you are following or from TV channels. You have put in so much time, and think this stock is going to go to the sky. You get greedy and invest more than your intended risk of 1R or 1%. Suppose you are so sure, you open a position with a 10R or 10% risk, and the stock goes against you. What happens? Instead of a 1R loss, you now have a 10R loss. This was purely because you got greedy. So always remember not to risk more than 1% on any given trade.

Another reason why this emotion could occur is when you have a string of winners; let us say you have 5 consecutive winners making you 3R wins each. Then you project this into the future, thinking the next trade will also be the same. And instead of risking the same 1R, you have now risked 5R, only to realize that it was a losing trade. So instead of losing 1R, you have lost 5R. This is when you discover that sticking to your objectives could have avoided both of these situations. There is a Wall Street saying, "Bulls make money, bears make money, but pigs get slaughtered because they are greedy." So don't get greedy.

SITUATION 2: FEAR

When you don't have your SL and TP orders in place, what usually happens is you will get uncontrolled losses, and when the profits do occur, you are not able to let them run. You want to take small profits because you are fearful that these profits will be lost. Remember, in trading, you will go broke if you take small profits and let your losses run. So make sure to open positions with a maximum risk of 1%, and let your winning trades reach their full profit potential of 3R or more, else you will go broke. Sticking to your objectives will save you from disaster.

SITUATION 3: HOPE

When you open a position and it goes against you, you should make sure that you close your position at a maximum 1R risk.

When you place an order without an SL, and the price starts dipping to 1R, 2R, 5R, and then 10R (I have done this when I was a rookie), you don't close the position because you are hoping for the trade to turn back around. As I have said earlier, when it comes to trading, Hope is for the hopeless. So stop hoping and make sure to place SL orders and TP orders while you are entering a trade. Take your losses at manageable planned intervals. Don't hope for a losing position to turn around, they rarely do.

HANDLING CONSECUTIVE LOSERS:

There have been many simulations done in the past with a trading system that produces 50% winners. There are times where you can have 16 – 20 consecutive losses, and this can be really devastating times. If you risked 5% or more on these trades, you'd have gone broke. So make sure you risk no more than 1% on any position, and a maximum cumulative risk of 10R. This will save you during devastating times. Without capital, you are not a trader. So do not lose your capital.

Imagine you have 9 losses in a row, you think the 10th trade will be a profitable one. Now you get edgy and risk 25R, but it turns out to be a losing trade. How would you feel? What should you have done to avoid this loss? Think and feel these emotions. To be a successful pro trader, you have to be able to take your losing trades well. It's part of the game. There is no Holy Grail system that will produce all winning trades. If someone says they have 90% winning trades, ask them how much they lost on their 10% losing trades. Obviously, if your TP is really small and your SL is really big, you get these 90% winners. But are they in line with your objectives? Think.

The biggest competitor or enemy in this business is not the markets, or hedge funds, or large institutions, it is your emotions. If you follow your objectives and respect the rules of the game, making money will be an effortless process. At the same time, risk too much, and you will be making mistakes one after the other, your statements will not show that you are growing your account consistently.

I differentiate a professional trader from a Rookie trader based on the below qualities.

PROFESSIONAL TRADER	ROOKIE TRADER
It's a business; is here to make money.	It's a hobby; here to have some fun.
Trades based on trading plan and objective.	Trades based on emotions, tips, recommendations. Has no sense of strategy or objective.
Always thinking of what can be lost in the trade.	Always looking at the possible wins only.
Enters the trade based on valid signals.	Enters randomly, just to prove to be a trader.
Knows when to exit, so he/she always has a TAKE PROFIT and STOP LOSS order.	Has no sense of when to exit, either with a loss or profit.
Risks a maximum of 1% of the account on any given trade.	No set risk percentage; no calculations; here to gamble recklessly.

Doesn't celebrate wins or losses.	Celebrates wins and depresses over losses.
Only thinks in terms of 'R' multiples.	Greedy behavior ensures overtrading.
No mood swings as everything is calculated.	Huge mood swings, as nothing is calculated.
Has a cumulative risk of 10% maximum on the total equity.	Exposes more than 10% of equity, expecting to get rich quick.
Responsible for their actions.	Constantly blaming anything and everything for their stupid mistakes.
Cuts losers short at predefined levels, and lets winners run to full profit potential.	Lets losers run and hope for them to turn back up. And cuts winners short to have instant gratification.
Thinks as the owner of a casino.	Thinks as the player in a casino.

CHAPTER 5

CONTINGENCIES AND RISKS

In trading, anything can happen at any time, I want to give you an idea of things that will go wrong when you are trading. Make sure you have all these covered to avoid unwanted surprises. You can never predict when they are coming, so always plan for the worst.

5A. GAP DOWN

You may have the best of strategies, but you will face sudden gap downs in price. Meaning the price could have jumped down without touching your SL.

Example: You buy a stock at $20 with a 10% SL at $18 and TP at $26.00. But then there is some bad news overnight or during the weekend. And the next morning, the stock opens at $16. Now your initial risk of 1R has become 2R. You followed your objectives but this can still happen, and some brokers close the position. But some don't. So make sure you immediately close the position. Don't wait and hope for it to turn back up. Whatever the loss, take it and get out of the position. This will be an unplanned loss in your trading journal. I try to avoid this situation by choosing brokers that offer a guaranteed stop. It means if the price jumps my SL, my position is closed at my planned SL with only a 1R. The catch is that there is a small premium that you have to pay. I add this to my initial risk itself. You can read many articles online about this. Just a few years back when the Swiss franc (CHF) suddenly gapped down because of a decision, its government took over the weekend to unpeg the Swiss franc (CHF) against the Euro (EUR). Many traders lost their entire life savings. And traders, who were trading using leveraged products without any guaranteed stops, went bankrupt overnight. This even included a few brokers.

5B. SPIKES THAT KILL

Rookies place really tight SL orders. I usually place my stops 5%-7% below my opening price. Anything below that, I consider to be tight. There are some exceptions based on the trading strategy. The stocks that I trade are also traded by big hedge funds. They have ample software to see where others' SL orders are placed. They will feed on these SL orders to get better rates. You don't want to have too tight SL orders; the price could suddenly fall 2% to 3% and turn back around to the upside. If you had a tight stop, your position would have been closed. You were right about the stock but wrong in placing an SL. So make sure to give your stock enough space to breathe. A 7% to 10% SL order is a good start. Mind you, this should be maximum only 1% of your trading capital.

5C. LOSERS COME FIRST

Even with the best of strategies, there will be losing trades. During the first few days to weeks, you will see a small dip in your equity curve. Only then will the profitable trades will start driving the equity curve up. So don't immediately assume that your strategy is not good. If you change it, you will face it again and again, so relax and stick to a proven strategy. If you have a 15% drop with no winning trades at all to your equity by following the rules of the strategy, only then should you re-evaluate the strategy. Usually, with about 10 open positions, a good strategy will have at least 3 – 4 profitable trades. It's a variable that you need to take into account while trading.

5D. BROKERS & SLIPPAGE

Slippage is when a broker offers you a bad price, it may be off by just a few cents, and it can be the opening price, or the SL or TP. That is a sign of a bad broker. Over the long run, you can lose a significant part of your profit to slippage. Choosing a broker that fits your trading style is essential to your success. There are brokers who bet the opposite of your positions. Some brokers charge exorbitant commissions, with really wide spreads. And sometimes, brokers can even go bankrupt; you could lose your entire life savings in cases like this.

Do your research and find the brokers that are genuinely good. Make sure they are regulated by the proper authorities. If you are choosing leveraged products, you should understand the risks involved before trading. If you are from certain countries, you can trade by spread betting or CFD. These products will accelerate your growth, but at the same time, you could lose even more money than your initial deposit. Be wise, and choose your broker and trading vehicle correctly. I do not recommend any particular brokers for various reasons. You should make sure to do your due diligence before choosing a broker.

5E. EXPERT ADVISORS (EA)

Expert Advisors or EAs are automated trading software. There are many of them available online. I have tried 100s of them, and none of them fit me. I don't know the rules of how they are built or what strategies they use to buy and sell. I cannot vouch for any of them. I believe these EAs are a big scam in the financial markets. There are many free ones in different blogs and some costing $1,000s of dollars. I don't bother using them at all.

5F. BINARY OPTIONS AND OTC MARKETS

In the world of trading, I believe that binary options are the biggest scams. Most of these companies work from shell companies offshore, so you can never trace where your money is. And the odds for binary options are so bad, it is like the casino where you cannot bend the rules. There is a time factor in your trades, and also, the payouts are below the dollar amount you risk, i.e. you make less than $1 for every $1 you risk. I have never traded the [OTC (Over the counter)](#) markets. Based on my research, buying stocks in OTC markets can be risky, they are not really regulated properly. There can be dummy companies with no products, no employees, and traded by insiders who try to scam money from the vulnerable. These products will have advertisements flashing everywhere on your computer. Please make sure to block these sites. They can be really deceptive. Especially now most of your search online is going to be about trading. Make sure not to get scammed.

5G. TRADING JOURNAL LAYOUT

As a successful pro trader, you should always have a trading journal; it helps you maintain records of your trades. You can analyze them while in profit and loss and spot the mistakes in your trading and correct them. Columns like date; time; day, and emotions can also be added to have a database to analyze and improve your performance. Trading is a business, and like all businesses, make sure you maintain a trading journal.

STOCK	ENTRY PRICE	INITIAL SL	RISK/SHARE	EQUITY % RISK	NUMBER OF SHARES	SELLING PRICE	PROFIT/LOSS	R MULTIPLE
A	$15	$12	$3	1	33	$12	-100	-1R
B	$20	$18	$2	1	50	$26	+300	+3R
C	$25	$20	$5	1	20	$20	-100	-1R
D	$10	$8	$2	1	50	$8	-100	-1R
E	$50	$46	$4	1	25	$62	+300	+3R
F	$45	$40	$5	1	20	$60	+300	+3R

Conclusion

We have learned how the business model of a casino makes money consistently over a period of time. I have shown you four strategies that I use day in day out to pick stocks that fit my personality and my trading style. I have shared my objectives, and what I expect from my trading business. By now, you should also be able to understand that taking a loss is part of the game. It's just like cutting out the dead part of the plant and giving room for the healthy part to grow. I let my winners run for at least three times average loss, so that even with just 50% odds, I make money consistently. I have shown you how controlling my risk and sticking to my objectives helps me keep my emotions in check. Now you know my secret combination of strategies I use to make money consistently from the stock market.

Another way I can put this is when you have a stock with good fundamentals, strong technical signs, your emotions are in line with your objectives, and you have the confidence to pull the trigger, you are bound to make money. Always approach trading with caution; by controlling your risk, you will begin a fruitful journey in the markets. A good trade is not when you have made or lost money, it is when you have followed the rules religiously. If you still have doubts and questions, you can contact me on stockmagnatebook@gmail.com. I hope you enjoyed reading the book as much I enjoyed writing it. It would really mean a lot to me if you can take the time to write a review on Amazon, even a short review helps.

References and Reading list

1. Reminiscences of a stock operator by Edwin Lefevre – 1923
2. How To Trade In Stocks by Jesse Livermore – 1940
3. How I Made $2,000,000 in the Stock Market by Nicolas Darvas –1960
4. Market Wizards by Jack D Schwager – 1989
5. The New Market Wizards by Jack D Schwager –1992
6. Stock Market Wizards by Jack D Schwager –2001
7. How to Make Money in Stocks – A Winning System in Good Times Or Bad by William J O'Neil –2009
8. Definitive Guide to Position Sizing Strategies by Dr. Van Tharp – 2013

Websites:

1. http://mam.econoday.com/ (This website shows upcoming market moving events)
2. http://www.investors.com/
3. https://marketsmith.investors.com/
4. http://www.finviz.com/
5. http://www.MARKETINOUT.COM

www.ingramcontent.com/pod-product-compliance
Lightning Source LLC
Chambersburg PA
CBHW070309230526
45470CB00002B/793